W9-APJ-384

Fall

Judy Wearing

W WEIGL PUBLISHERS INC.
"Creating Inspired Learning"
www.weigl.com

Published by Weigl Publishers Inc.
350 5th Avenue, 59th Floor
New York, NY 10118
Website: www.weigl.com

Library of Congress Cataloging-in-Publication Data

Wearing, Judy.
 Fall : WOW study of day and seasons / Judy Wearing.
     p. cm.
 Includes bibliographical references and index.
 ISBN 978-1-61690-044-1 (hardcover : alk. paper) -- ISBN 978-1-61690-048-9 (softcover : alk. paper) -- ISBN 978-1-61690-052-6 (e-book : alk. paper)
 1. Autumn--Juvenile literature. I. Title.
 QB637.7.W43 2011
 508.2--dc22

                              2009050310

Printed in the United States of America in North Mankato, Minnesota
1 2 3 4 5 6 7 8 9 0 14 13 12 11 10

042010
WEP264000

Editor: Heather C. Hudak
Design: Terry Paulhus

All of the Internet URLs given in the book were valid at the time of publication. However, due to the dynamic nature of the Internet, some addresses may have changed, or sites may have ceased to exist since publication. While the author and publisher regret any inconvenience this may cause readers, no responsibility for any such changes can be accepted by either the author or the publisher.

Every reasonable effort has been made to trace ownership and to obtain permission to reprint copyright material. The publishers would be pleased to have any errors or omissions brought to their attention so that they may be corrected in subsequent printings.

Weigl acknowledges Getty Images as its primary image supplier for this title.

CONTENTS

What is Fall?

How do you know when summer break is over? The days are shorter, and the warmth of summer begins to turn cold. This is fall. Fall is the season before winter. It is a time of change.

Fall brings rain, cool breezes, and colorful leaves. The fall season is also called autumn.

When it is spring in North America, countries south of the **equator** have fall.

Cool and Crisp

Did you know that nighttime is a little longer in fall? Fall days are shorter than summer days. The sunshine is less bright, and the sky gets dark earlier.

Fall weather is crisp. There are many sunny days, but the air is cool. There is more rain in fall than in summer.

In Barrow, Alaska, the Sun sets in November and does not rise again until late January.

Ready for Winter

How do you get ready for winter? Do you put on a heavy sweater? Fall is the season when plants and animals get ready for winter. Some animals grow a thick coat of fur to stay warm.

To get ready for winter, many animals find a place to live. Squirrels may hide in holes in tree trunks, and some bears hide in caves. Turtles and frogs burrow in mud at the bottom of ponds.

Like leaves, some animals change color in fall. The brown summer coat of the weasel turns white. This helps it blend with the snow.

A Fall Home

Did you know that blue whales swim south in fall? These huge mammals travel thousands of miles (kilometers) to spend the winter in warmer waters. They eat almost no food during this time. Once at their winter home, blue whales mate and give birth. In spring, the whales return to colder waters. There, they spend three to four months eating.

In fall, many birds leave their summer homes to find warmer places to live. The Arctic **tern** is a type of bird that lives in the Arctic. Each fall, Arctic terns travel to Antarctica. The journey takes three months.

Changing Colors

What happens to tree leaves in fall? They change from green to yellow, red, and brown.

Chlorophyll uses sunlight to make food for plants. It also makes leaves green. In fall, there is less sunlight, so chlorophyll fades away. With less chlorophyll, leaves begin to look less green. They appear more yellow.

Sunshine makes the yellow colors in leaves look orange and red. The more sunshine there is, the brighter red the leaves become.

Harvest Time

Have you ever seen a bright, reddish full Moon that seems to take up more room in the sky? In September, the Moon rises at or near sunset. It hangs lower in the sky, making it look larger than at other times of the year. This "**harvest** Moon" provides light for farmers working late at night to harvest their **crops**.

Many fruits and vegetables are ready to be picked in fall. These include apples, pumpkins, beets, brussel sprouts, and turnips. Corn and wheat also are ready to harvest in fall.

Pumpkin Period

Why do some people think pumpkins are a sign of fall? When Europeans came to North America, they saw American Indians eating pumpkins. Soon, these squash became a part of settlers' meals. Today, pies, soups, muffins, and other treats are made from pumpkins.

The largest known pumpkin weighed 1,700 pounds (771 kilograms). This is as much as a small car.

Happy Halloween

Do you celebrate Halloween? Halloween takes place on October 31 each year. Children wear costumes, and people decorate their houses. They cut shapes in pumpkins and put a candle inside to make the pumpkin glow. These pumpkins are called Jack o' lanterns.

Each year, farmers in the United States grow about 1 billion pounds (450 million kilograms) of pumpkin.

Thanksgiving

Does your family eat turkey on Thanksgiving? After fall harvest, there usually is plenty of food. To celebrate, people take a day off work and have a special meal. In the United States, this holiday is called Thanksgiving. It takes place on the fourth Thursday of November each year. Turkey, cranberries, potatoes, stuffing, and pumpkin pie are common Thanksgiving foods.

The pilgrims celebrated the first Thanksgiving in 1621, in Plymouth, Massachusetts. The Wampanoag Indians had taught the pilgrims how to harvest. They were invited to the Thanksgiving event. It lasted three days.

Fall Colors

Supplies

small jar with a lid

chopped frozen spinach

rubbing alcohol

a long strip of
coffee filter paper

tablespoon

1. Put a tablespoon of spinach into the jar. With an adult's help, pour rubbing alcohol into the jar until it covers the spinach.

2. Put the lid on the jar, and swirl it gently. Leave the jar still for an hour. Swirl it again, and leave it for another hour.

3. Take the lid off the jar. Put one end of the paper into the spinach mix.

4. Leave the paper in the spinach mix for an hour. Then, let the paper dry.

5. What colors do you see on the paper? Can you see green or yellow?

6. Next, cut two leaves into tiny pieces, and repeat the steps using them in place of the spinach. What colors do you see?

Find Out More

To learn more about fall, visit these websites.

BrainPOP
www.brainpop.com/
science/weather/
seasons/preview.weml

PBS Kids Go!
http://pbskids.org/dragon
flytv/show/leaves.html

National Geographic Kids
http://kids.national
geographic.com/Stories/
History/First-thanksgiving

The History Channel
www.history.com/
content/halloween

Glossary

chlorophyll: the green substance in plants that changes energy from the Sun into sugar for the plant to use to grow

crops: plants that are grown by farmers to be sold

equator: the imaginary line around the middle of the globe; the halfway point between the North Pole and the South Pole

harvest: to gather crops; crops that have been gathered

tern: a type of bird that is related to seagulls and lives near the ocean

Index